I am Dot. I am a big dog.

I am Dash. I am a little dog.

Dash can see a bee on Dot.

Buzz... Zzzz.

Dot jumps up. A bee!

Dot can see the bee.

Dot runs off.

Dash jumps up. Go, Dash, go! Get the bee!

Dash runs. Dash jumps.

Dash cannot get the bee.

The dogs sit on the grass.
Oh no! The bee is back.